Sinbad

T0116757

BEFORE READING

1 This is Sinbad. Where does he come from?

a ☐ Athens

b ☐ Baghdad

c ☐ Istanbul

d ☐ Egypt

2 Sinbad meets many people and animals in different countries. Here are some of them. Match the sentences with the pictures and find out their names.

1 He is a rich man.
2 They eat people.
3 They are long, and can eat big animals.
4 She is the beautiful daughter of a king.
5 She is the prisoner of a monster.
6 They are very big birds.

a ☐ **Rocs**

b ☐ **Snakes**

c ☐ **Cannibals**

d ☐ **The King of Serendib**

e ☐ **Ayisha**

f ☐ **Yasmin**

3 Answer these questions about the people and animals in Activity 2.

a Who does Sinbad fall in love with? ....
b Who does Sinbad run away from? ....
c Who does Sinbad help? ....
d Who helps Sinbad? ....,...............

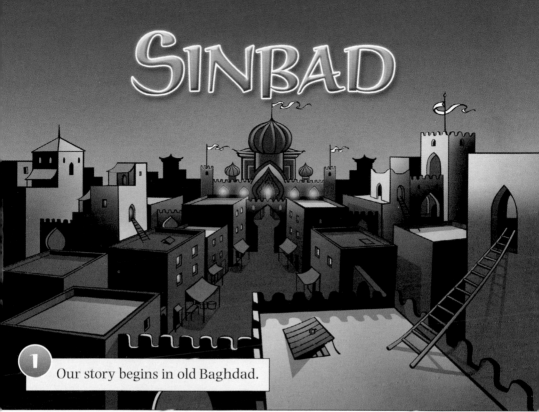

1 Our story begins in old Baghdad.

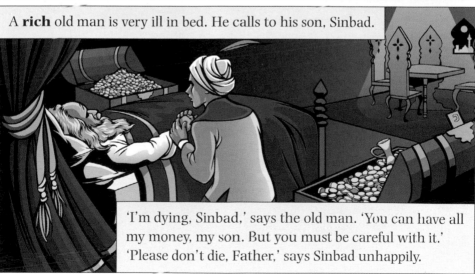

A **rich** old man is very ill in bed. He calls to his son, Sinbad.

'I'm dying, Sinbad,' says the old man. 'You can have all my money, my son. But you must be careful with it.'
'Please don't die, Father,' says Sinbad unhappily.

rich with a lot of money

Sinbad's father dies, and Sinbad is unhappy for a long time.
But one day he thinks: 'I'm a very **lucky** man. I have a lot of money now, some beautiful things, and a big house.'

With his father's money, Sinbad **buys** new things to wear . . .

. . . and expensive things to eat from the **market**.

Every evening Sinbad's friends come to his house. They eat and drink all night.

lucky when something happens that is good for you

buy to give money for something

market where people go to buy things in the street

But after a year, Sinbad has no more money.

Every day angry **shopkeepers** come to Sinbad's house.
'Where's our money?' they ask angrily.

Sinbad goes to the market, and he **sells** his father's best tables and chairs. With the money he buys some beautiful **carpets**.

'I can **sail** to different countries,' Sinbad thinks. 'And I can sell these carpets for a lot of money. Then I can give the money back to the shopkeepers.'

Next, Sinbad finds an old **ship** with a very old **captain**.

shopkeeper a person who has a small shop

sell to take money for something

carpet a piece of thick material that you put on the floor

sail to go across the water

ship you use a ship to go across the water

captain the most important person on a ship

Three days later Sinbad is ready to leave Baghdad. He talks excitedly to all the **sailors** on the ship. 'I want to bring back a lot of money,' he tells them.

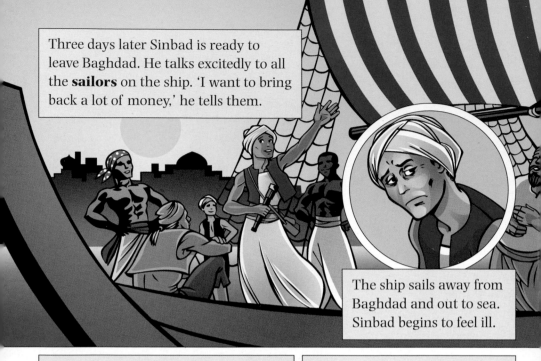

The ship sails away from Baghdad and out to sea. Sinbad begins to feel ill.

After two days at sea, Sinbad is very ill. But then he sees a beautiful **island**. 'Please stop!' he says to the captain.

Sinbad and some of the sailors **land** on the island. Sinbad takes a **barrel** with him. He wants to look for water. The captain stays on the ship.

sailor a man who works on a ship
island a country in the sea

land to arrive from a ship or from the air

barrel a tall round box; you put things to drink in it

Sinbad and the sailors are all very happy. 'What a wonderful island!' says Sinbad. 'Let's sit down and make a **fire**.'

They sit near the fire and they begin to sing. Suddenly the island moves. 'The island is moving!' says Sinbad.
'This isn't an island,' cry the sailors. 'It's a **whale**!'

Sinbad quickly gets into the barrel. The whale moves down into the water. All the sailors are now in the sea. 'Help! Help!' they cry.

Now it is dark, and Sinbad is at sea in the barrel.
'Hello! Hello!' he cries.
But nobody answers.

fire this is red and hot and it burns   **whale** a very big animal that lives in the sea and looks like a fish

5

ACTIVITIES

READING CHECK

Are these sentences true or false? Tick the boxes.　　True　False

a Sinbad's father is ill and he dies. ☑ ☐

b Sinbad is careful with his father's money. ☐ ☐

c The shopkeepers are very angry with Sinbad. ☐ ☐

d Sinbad buys tables and chairs at the market. ☐ ☐

e Sinbad sails to an island in a nice new ship. ☐ ☐

f The island is a whale. ☐ ☐

g Sinbad gets into a barrel. ☐ ☐

h The captain of the ship finds Sinbad in the barrel. ☐ ☐

WORD WORK

1 Find nine more words from Chapter 1 in the wordsquare.

2 Use the words from Activity 1 to complete the sentences.

a She's very . . . . . rich . . . . . and she lives in a big house in Hollywood.

b They live on a small . . . . in the Mediterranean Sea.

c We haven't got any money so we can't . . . . that new TV.

d It's cold today. Let's make a . . . .

e My father works at sea – he's a . . . .

f It's OK to walk on this old . . . . in your shoes.

g He's . . . . He has everything – a nice family and an interesting job.

h This is a big bookshop. They . . . . lots of books every day.

i We love the sea. We go everywhere by . . . . and we always . . . . in interesting countries.

3 Match the words with the pictures.

> **barrel captain market sail ~~shopkeeper~~ whale**

a shopkeeper

b . . . .

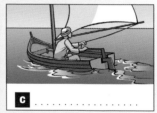

c . . . .

d . . . .

e . . . .

f . . . .

GUESS WHAT

What happens in the next chapter? Tick two boxes.

a ☐ Sinbad finds the ship again.

b ☐ Sinbad lands on a small island.

c ☐ A Roc takes Sinbad up into the sky.

d ☐ A snake eats Sinbad.

2 The next morning Sinbad looks out of the barrel. He is now **alone** on a small island. Far away he can see a big white **stone**.

He goes to the stone and he looks carefully at it. 'What's this?' he thinks.

Suddenly the sky **becomes** black. Sinbad feels very afraid. 'Help! What's happening?' he cries. He looks up at the sky. A very big **bird** is **flying** nearer and nearer.

He begins to run away. 'Now I understand!' he thinks, 'That bird is a Roc, and that big white stone is a Roc's **egg**.'

alone with nobody

stone something grey or white, and hard

become to change from one thing to a different thing

bird an animal that can fly through the sky

fly to move through the air

egg a round thing with a young bird inside it

The Roc sits on the egg and then it goes to sleep. Sinbad takes off his **turban** and he puts it **around** the Roc's leg. 'When the Roc flies away, I can leave the island too,' he thinks.

In the morning, the Roc flies away. Sinbad flies up into the sky with the bird.

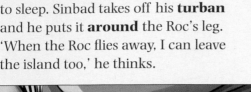

The Roc flies for hours and hours. In the end, it flies down into a **valley** and lands there.

turban something that you wear on your head

around all the way round

valley land between two hills

Sinbad finds lots of little stones in the valley. 'What are these?' he thinks. 'I know!' he cries. 'They're **jewels**!' And he puts some of them in his bag.

Then he hears a noise.

There are three big **snakes** behind him. He runs away very fast. In front of him he sees lots of dead **animals** in the valley.

'Oh, no, the snakes kill everything here!' he thinks.

He goes behind one of the dead animals and he waits. Suddenly a Roc flies down and takes the dead animal up into the sky.

Sinbad quickly puts his arms around the dead animal. He flies up into the sky with the Roc. 'Where am I going now?' he thinks.

---

jewel a very expensive stone

snake a long animal with no legs

animal a living being that can think and move

The Roc flies out of the valley and it lands near a village. The men from the village run to see it, and the Roc flies away. Sinbad comes out from under the dead animal.
'Who are you?' ask the men.
'I'm Sinbad the Sailor,' says Sinbad. 'Would you like to buy these jewels from the valley?'

The men are **surprised**. 'Nobody goes into the valley,' they say. 'The snakes eat everything there.'
'Not me!' laughs Sinbad.
'You're very lucky!' say the men.

The people from the village buy Sinbad's jewels. He's a rich man now, and he wants to go back to Baghdad. 'We can find a ship for you,' say the people from the village.

In Baghdad Sinbad gives money to the shopkeepers.
'Are you truly Sinbad?' they ask.
'Yes!' he says. And he tells them about his **adventures**.

surprised feeling that something very new is suddenly happening

adventure something very exciting that happens to you

READING CHECK

Match the two parts of the sentences.

a Sinbad lands on . . .   1 the shopkeepers.

b The big white stone is . . .   2 the people from the village.

c The Roc takes Sinbad up into . . .   3 an island.

d The Roc lands in . . .   4 Baghdad.

e Sinbad runs away from . . .   5 a Roc's egg.

f Sinbad sells his jewels to . . .   6 the snakes.

g Sinbad sails back to . . .   7 a valley.

h Sinbad gives the money back to . . .   8 the sky.

WORD WORK

1 Find words from Chapter 2 in the snake.

alone turban stones becomes bird around animals adventure surprised jewels

2 Use the words from Activity 1 to complete the sentences.

a Sinbad can't find any of the sailors. He's .... *alone* .....

b Sinbad always wears a .... on his head.

c A Roc is a very big ....

d When the Roc flies over Sinbad, the sky .... black.

e In the valley there are a lot of dead ....

f When Sinbad arrives in the valley, he sees some small ....
They are .... When Sinbad understands this, he puts them in his bag.

g In the village the men stand .... Sinbad and they ask him questions.

h Sinbad tells the men about the valley and they are all very ....

GUESS WHAT

What does Sinbad do in the next chapter? Read the sentences and write *Yes* or *No*.

a Sinbad stays at home in Baghdad. He becomes very poor. .....

b Sinbad needs some money. He buys some more carpets and he sails away in a ship. .....

c Sinbad goes to an island. A Roc wants to kill him. .....

d Sinbad sells a lot of carpets. He becomes rich. .....

3 Sinbad's friends come to visit him at his father's house. But there is nothing to eat or drink, and the house is dirty. His friends soon go away.

'I need more money,' he thinks. 'Then I can have a beautiful house again.'

The next morning Sinbad finds a ship and a captain. He buys lots of things at the market, and he puts them on the ship. He's ready to leave Baghdad again.

After a week at sea, there is a big **storm**. Sinbad is ill, and he stays in bed. After the storm, the ship arrives at an island.

'That's the island of Zugab,' says the captain.

Sinbad is very excited. 'Perhaps I can sell my things to people on the island,' he thinks.

storm a lot of rain and very bad weather

Sinbad **explores** the island with two of the sailors. They find lots of jewels there.

Just then, a big **wave** hits the ship. The wave takes the ship far out to sea.

Sinbad and the two sailors are very afraid, so they **climb** behind some big stones. When night comes, they go to sleep.

In the morning they find a big snake around them. The snake eats one of the sailors.

explore to walk around a new country and learn about it

wave a line of water that moves across the top of the sea

climb to go up or down using your hands and feet

Quickly Sinbad and the second sailor climb a tree. They stay there all day and all night.

When Sinbad **wakes up** in the morning, he's alone. 'Oh no! The second sailor is dead too,' he thinks. 'And I'm the snake's next breakfast!' Just then, Sinbad sees some **wood** near the tree.

Sinbad climbs down the tree and he makes some **armour** from the wood. Then he sees the snake. The snake is hungry.

Sinbad stays in his armour all night. The snake moves around him, but it can't eat Sinbad.

wake up to stop sleeping

wood the hard part of a tree

armour when you wear this, people cannot kill you

16

In the morning Sinbad wakes up.
'Where's the snake?' he thinks.
The snake is sleeping in the sun
near the tree.
Then, Sinbad sees a ship out at
sea. 'I know that ship,' he thinks.
'It's my old ship!'

Sinbad quietly climbs out of the
armour, and quickly puts some
jewels in his bag.
Then he runs to the sea. The snake
wakes up and comes after Sinbad.
But Sinbad runs faster and gets to
the sea before the snake can eat him.

Sinbad swims to the ship.
'It's Sinbad!' cry the sailors. 'You're
a very lucky man! We have all your
beautiful carpets from Baghdad!'
'Thank you!' says Sinbad.

The ship sails home. It stops at
lots of different countries and
Sinbad sells all his carpets. When
he arrives in Baghdad, he has a
lot of money.

READING CHECK

Choose the right words to finish the sentences.

a Sinbad needs more money because he wants to have a beautiful . . .
1 ☑ house.
2 ☐ table.

b There's a storm at sea and Sinbad feels very . . .
1 ☐ afraid.
2 ☐ ill.

c On Zugab, Sinbad finds lots of . . .
1 ☐ jewels.
2 ☐ people.

d Sinbad and the sailors climb a . . .
1 ☐ big stone.
2 ☐ tree.

e The snake eats . . .
1 ☐ two sailors.
2 ☐ three sailors.

f Sinbad makes . . .
1 ☐ a house.
2 ☐ some armour.

g Sinbad runs away from . . .
1 ☐ the captain of the ship.
2 ☐ the snake.

h Sinbad comes home with a lot of . . .
1 ☐ carpets.
2 ☐ money.

WORD WORK

1 Find words from Chapter 6 in the carpets.

a w o o d   **b** c _ _ _ _   **c** w _ _ _ _   **d** a _ _ _ _ _

e e _ _ _ _ _ _   **f** w _ _ _ _ _   **g** s _ _ _ _

2 Use words from Activity 1 to complete the sentences.

a Let's find some . . . wood . . . . . . and make a big fire.

b Don't go in the sea. There are a lot of big . . . .

c This is an interesting old house. I'd like to . . . . all the rooms in it.

d It's seven o'clock! It's time to . . . . now and have breakfast!

e The sky is very black. A bad . . : . . . . is coming, I think.

f You can . . . . up that small tree. It's very easy.

g In this old picture the king is wearing some grey . . . .

GUESS WHAT

What happens in the next chapter? Tick two boxes.

Sinbad . . .

a ☐ goes to sea again for more adventures.

b ☐ stays in Baghdad and writes about his adventures.

c ☐ meets a beautiful woman and marries her.

d ☐ goes back to the island of Zugab and gets more jewels.

4 Sinbad's friends are very happy to see him. Sinbad tells them all about his adventures.

But after some time Sinbad is not happy in Baghdad. 'I want to go back to sea,' he tells his friends.

A week later, Sinbad leaves Baghdad on a big, tall ship. He's very excited. 'It's time for some more adventures,' he tells the captain.

The ship sails for three weeks. But one night there's a storm. The ship **breaks** here and there, and it must land.

In the morning the ship lands near a **beach**. Sinbad and some of the sailors go to find help.

break to go into little pieces   **beach** the land next to the sea

They meet some **strange** men on the beach. 'Hello. Can you help us?' Sinbad asks them. But the strange men don't understand.

Suddenly the men take Sinbad and the sailors to their village. Sinbad is now very afraid. 'Oh no! They're **cannibals**,' he thinks.

The cannibals put the sailors and Sinbad in a **cage**. They give the sailors lots of good things to eat. The sailors are very hungry. Sinbad is hungry too, but he eats nothing.

Soon the sailors are fat, and the cannibals are very hungry. That evening they take the fattest sailor and eat him. The next day they take one more sailor.

strange not usual

cannibal a person who eats people

cage an open box to put animals or people in

'I must get out,' thinks Sinbad. Sinbad is very **thin** and he can get through the cage easily. That evening, when the cannibals eat their dinner, Sinbad runs away.

The next morning, Sinbad arrives in a new country. He sees some people. 'Are they cannibals, too?' thinks Sinbad.
But these people are not cannibals. They take Sinbad to their **king**.

Sinbad tells the king about his wonderful adventures. The king listens carefully.
'You're a lucky man,' he says. 'You can make us lucky too. You must **marry** my daughter, Ayisha.'

When Sinbad sees Ayisha's beautiful face, he **falls in love with** her at once.
Sinbad marries Ayisha in front of the king and all the people.

thin not fat

king the most important man in a country

marry to make someone your wife or husband

fall in love with to begin to love someone

A year after the wedding, Ayisha becomes ill. A friend talks to Sinbad quietly.
'Be careful! When a woman dies in this country, they **bury** the **husband** with her,' he says.
'What?' cries Sinbad.
Ayisha becomes very ill, and in the end she dies.

The king buries Sinbad with Ayisha. He also buries lots of jewels with them. Sinbad is now far under the **ground**.

Sinbad waits to die. But suddenly he sees an animal near him. It's a big, strange animal. Sinbad puts lots of jewels in his bag and he quickly **follows** the animal through the ground.

bury to put a dead person under the ground

husband the man that a woman marries

ground we walk on this

follow to go after something or somebody

ACTIVITIES

READING CHECK

Put these sentences in the correct order. Number them 1–8.

a ☐ Sinbad becomes very thin and he can get through the easily.

b ☐ Sinbad marries but she dies.

c ☐ There's a and the ship lands near a beach.

d ☐ Sinbad arrives in a new country and he meets the .

e ☐ Sinbad leaves Baghdad on a tall .

f ☐ The king buries with Ayisha.

g ☐ The king wants Sinbad to his daughter, Ayisha.

h ☐ Sinbad meets some and they put him in a cage.

WORD WORK

Use the words in the ship to complete the sentences.

a 'Where's the nearest supermarket?'

'. . . . Follow. . . . me. It's near here.'

b 'It's very hot today.'

'Yes, let's go down to the sea and sit on the

. . . .'

c 'Can I see your new watch?'

'Yes, but please don't . . . . it.'

d 'This is my . . . . His name is Mark.'

'Nice to meet you.'

e 'Is that your brother?'

'Yes, he's the tall, ... boy with dark hair.'

f 'Can you hear that . . . . noise?'

'Yes, my cat is calling me. She wants to come in!'

g 'Look at your white coat. It's on the . . . .'

'Oh no. It's very dirty now.'

h 'I love Sharon.'

'Oh no, not Sharon! You always . . . . the wrong girls!'

i 'This animal is ill and it can't move.'

'Don't worry. Let's put it in the . . . . over there.'

break

thin strange

beach

ground husband

fall in love with

follow cage

GUESS WHAT

What happens in the next chapter? Tick one box.

a ☐ The king finds Sinbad and he's very angry.

b ☐ The king finds Sinbad. Sinbad marries the king's second daughter.

c ☐ Sinbad meets some sailors and he sails away on a ship.

d ☐ Sinbad meets the cannibals again. They put him back in the cage.

When Sinbad comes out from under the ground, he meets some sailors.
'I'm Sinbad the Sailor,' he tells them.
The sailors are surprised. 'Sinbad? But Sinbad is dead,' they say.
'Well, I'm not dead now!' Sinbad says. 'And I want to meet your captain.'

The sailors take Sinbad to their ship.
'Are you Sinbad the Sailor?' asks the captain.
'Yes,' says Sinbad.
'Then, sail with us and tell us about your adventures,' says the captain.

The ship sails for many weeks. One morning, the captain sees an island. Sinbad and some of the sailors land and begin to explore the island.

The sailors find a very big bird's egg. 'Don't touch it!' says Sinbad. 'It's a Roc's egg!'
But the sailors **throw** stones at the egg.

throw to make something move from your hand through the air

The egg breaks open and a big fat young Roc comes out. It makes a lot of noise. Suddenly four angry Rocs fly down. 'Let's go back to the ship!' says Sinbad.

The Rocs begin to **attack** the ship with big stones. 'We must sail away now!' cries the captain.

The ship sails into a bad storm, and Sinbad lands in the sea. After many hours in the water, he climbs onto some big stones near a beach.

Sinbad begins to explore. There are big, black stones all around the beach, and a big **cave** with a **river** in it. He finds the **wrecks** of old ships and hundreds of jewels on the beach.

attack to begin fighting

cave a big hole in the ground

river water that moves in a long line

wreck a very old broken ship

'More jewels!' says Sinbad, and he puts some of the beautiful stones in his bag.
Soon he begins to feel hungry. 'There are lots of jewels here,' he thinks. 'But there's nothing to eat. I must look for something. But where?'

Sinbad takes wood from the wrecks and makes a **boat** from it. He puts the boat on the river in the cave and gets on it.
He **rows** for days through the dark cave. He feels more and more hungry every day.

After six days, he's very ill and tired. But then he sees some blue sky. He can also see two strange men. 'Welcome to the country of Serendib!' they say.

'Please give me something to eat!' cries Sinbad. The men give Sinbad lots of different things, and he eats for hours.
'You're a lucky man,' say the men. 'Come with us to see our king.'

boat a little ship

row to move a boat through water using long pieces of wood

Sinbad gives some of the jewels to the king. He also tells him about the most important man in Baghdad, the **Caliph**. 'Your Caliph is a very good and **wise** man,' says the king. 'Here are some **presents** for him.'

The king finds a big ship for Sinbad and he gives him lots of presents, too. Sinbad sails back to Baghdad.

On the ship, he thinks about his adventure in the cave. 'This time I want to stay at home in Baghdad,' he thinks.

When Sinbad gives the presents to the Caliph of Baghdad, the Caliph says: 'I have some beautiful carpets for this wise King of Serendib. Please take them to him.' 'Oh, no!' thinks Sinbad. 'Back to sea again!'

caliph a very important man in an Arab country

wise when a person understands a lot about many things

present something that you give to someone

ACTIVITIES

READING CHECK

Choose the correct words to complete the sentences.

a Sinbad is **dead** ill , the sailors think.

b The sailors throw **wood** **stones** at the Roc's egg.

c The Rocs attack **the ship** **the island** .

d When Sinbad explores the beach he soon feels **tired** **hungry** .

e Sinbad makes a small **boat** **house** from the wood.

f Sinbad is in the dark cave for **two** **six** days.

g Sinbad tells the king about the **people** **Caliph** of Baghdad.

h The Caliph is a **wise** **bad** man, the King says.

i Sinbad sails back to Baghdad with **animals** **presents** for the Caliph.

j Sinbad wants to **stay at home** **go to sea** again.

WORD WORK

Use the pictures to write sentences with words from Chapter 5.

a I sometimes give to my friends.

I sometimes give presents to my friends.

b In the summer we often swim in the .

....

c It's very dark in this

....

d He can that  very fast.

· ·

e There's the of an old ship on a beach near here.

· ·

f Don't stones!

· ·

g Our dog people when they visit our house.

· ·

GUESS WHAT

What happens in the next chapter? Tick one box.

Sinbad . . .

a ☐ goes back to the country of Serendib and lives there for many years.

b ☐ dies after a sea monster attacks him.

c ☐ has more adventures at sea.

d ☐ becomes the Caliph of Baghdad.

6 Sinbad sails from Baghdad with the presents for the King of Serendib.

The King of Serendib is happy to see Sinbad again.
'Stay here!' he says to Sinbad. 'And tell me more about the wise Caliph of Baghdad.'

'I'm sorry,' says Sinbad. 'I must go back to Baghdad now. I'm tired of adventures.'

Sinbad begins to go home. One day, a sea **monster** attacks the ship.
'Help!' cries Sinbad. 'Not more adventures!'

monster an animal that is very bad to look at

The monster is angry. It eats some of the sailors from the ship. Quickly, Sinbad gets into a little boat and rows away.

Sinbad lands on an island. He leaves his boat on the beach, and goes to explore.

Sinbad finds a cave. He can hear a noise. 'Someone's crying,' he thinks. He looks into the cave and sees a young woman. In front of her, there's a monster. It is sleeping.
'She's the monster's **prisoner**,' thinks Sinbad. 'I must help her.'

Later, the monster leaves to look for something to eat. Sinbad goes into the cave.
'Who are you?' asks the woman.

'I'm Sinbad the Sailor,' he says. 'I can help you.'
'Thank you,' she says, 'I'm Yasmin.'

prisoner a person who is not free

Sinbad takes Yasmin to the boat on the beach.
'Can you row?' Sinbad asks her.
'Of course I can,' she says.
'Well, here's my boat. Let's row.'

Sinbad and Yasmin row all night. In the morning Sinbad sees his ship.

Sinbad and Yasmin climb up to the ship. 'Sinbad!' the sailors cry. 'You're alive!' 'Of course,' says Sinbad. 'And this is my friend, Yasmin.'

Just then, **pirates** attack the ship. The pirates make Sinbad and Yasmin their prisoners.

pirate a person on a ship who takes things from other ships

The pirates take Sinbad and Yasmin to a new country, and sell them to a man at the market. 'You must **hunt elephants** every day for their **ivory**,' says the man.

Sinbad and Yasmin are very good at hunting elephants.

One day, lots of elephants follow Sinbad and Yasmin. Yasmin is afraid. 'Why are those elephants following us?' she asks. 'It's all right,' says Sinbad. 'Elephants are very wise, you know. Perhaps they want to tell us something.'

hunt to look for and kill animals

elephant a very big animal with a long nose

ivory this is white and hard, and comes from the long tusks on an elephant's face

Sinbad and Yasmin climb a tree. The elephants are walking into a cave. 'Let's go into that cave,' says Sinbad.

In the cave Sinbad and Yasmin find lots of dead elephants. 'Look at all these dead elephants,' says Sinbad.

Sinbad takes the hunter to the dead elephants. The hunter is very happy. 'Thank you, Sinbad,' he says. 'Now we don't need to kill any elephants. We have lots of ivory here.'

'You can go now,' says the hunter, and he gives Sinbad and Yasmin a lot of money.

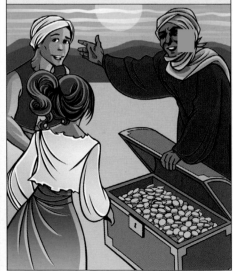

Sinbad and Yasmin sail back to Baghdad. Yasmin is very excited. 'I want to meet all your friends,' she says.

Sinbad takes Yasmin to his house. Yasmin is surprised. 'You're very rich!' she says.

'But money isn't the most important thing,' says Sinbad. 'We must help people, too.'

Sinbad then goes into the streets of Baghdad and he gives some of his money to the people there with no homes.
'Thank you, Sinbad!' they cry. 'You're a truly wise and good man.'

READING CHECK

Correct six more mistakes.

presents

Sinbad takes some ~~books~~ to the King of Serendib. After that Sinbad sails to Baghdad

but a Roc attacks his ship. Sinbad lands on an island and he finds an old woman.

Her name is Yasmin. Sinbad and Yasmin row in a boat to Sinbad's ship. Some pirates

attack the ship and Sinbad and Yasmin become their friends. The pirates sell Sinbad

and Yasmin to a hunter and they must hunt snakes every day. Sinbad and Yasmin find

a lot of jewels and they tell the hunter. The hunter gives them money and they go back

to Baghdad. Sinbad gives some of his carpets to poor people.

WORD WORK

1 These words don't match the pictures. Correct them.

a MONSTER

...pirate...

b ELEPHANT

. . . .

c PIRATE

. . . .

d HUNTER

. . . .

e IVORY

. . . .

f PRISONER

. . . .

2 Use the words from Activity 1 to complete the sentences.

a Sinbad becomes the cannibals' . . prisoner . ., but he runs away from them.

b I'm afraid to row on the river; a big green and black . . . . lives in the water!

c Can you see that . . . .? He's putting something to eat in his mouth with his long nose.

d . . . . is white and it's very expensive.

e There's a . . . . behind that tree. He wants to kill the animals over there.

f In the story of Peter Pan, Captain Hook is a . . . .; he wants to kill Peter Pan.

GUESS WHAT

**What happens to Sinbad after the end of the story?
Choose from these ideas or add your own.**

Sinbad . . .

a ☐ marries Yasmin. They have a lot of children.

b ☐ stays in Baghdad. He's very rich and he lives in a big house.

c ☐ gives all his money to poor people. He lives in a small house in Baghdad.

d ☐ stays in Baghdad for some time with Yasmin. But one day he leaves and goes back to sea.

e ☐ leaves Baghdad on a big ship. He dies in a storm.

f ☐ goes back to the country of Serendib. He becomes king there.

g ☐ . . . .

h ☐ . . . .

Project A   *Lucky or unlucky?*

1   **In the story Sinbad is a very lucky man. What is lucky or unlucky in England? Do you know? Complete the poster with the words from the box. Use your dictionary to help you.**

| black cat | coin | Friday the thirteenth |
| horseshoes | ladder | mirror | thirteen | well |

In England . . .

a   A . . . . is lucky.

b   Throwing money in a . . . . is lucky.

c   A . . . . is lucky.

d   Finding a little . . . . is lucky.

e   The number . . . . is unlucky.

f   Walking under a . . . . is unlucky.

g   Breaking a . . . . is unlucky.

h   . . . . is an unlucky day.

2 Look at the pictures. Are these things lucky or unlucky in your country? Or do they have no special meaning? Tick the box if it is the same in your country.

a ☐ People in Korea don't wash their hair before an exam because you wash away your memory, too, they say!

b ☐ Tuesday 13th is unlucky in Spain.

c ☐ A Turkish blue eye amulet keeps bad luck away.

d ☐ The number 4 is unlucky in Japan.

e ☐ People in Brazil always put the sugar in the cup before the coffee. This makes you rich, they think.

f ☐ In Italy black cats are unlucky.

3 What's lucky and unlucky in your country? Complete the table.

	LUCKY	UNLUCKY
ANIMAL		
THING		
DAY		
NUMBER		
THING TO DO		

4 Make a poster about lucky and unlucky things in your country.

Project B   *Dangerous activities*

1 Match the activities with the pictures. Use your dictionary to help you.

a ☐ snowboarding   **c** ☐ hang-gliding   **e** ☐ bungee-jumping

b ☐ climbing   **d** ☐ scuba diving   **f** ☐ white-water rafting

2 What activities are they talking about?

I'd like to go (a) . . . . I'm very good at rowing. I'm in the rowing club at school and we go rowing every Saturday. But the river isn't very exciting. I'd like to do something more dangerous.

I'd like to go (b) . . . . I'm not afraid of high places and I like being in the mountains. At school we practise on a wall. The wall isn't high, so it's very easy. I'd like to do something more difficult.

3 Which activity would you like to do? Explain why.

4 Read the advertisement about a course for a dangerous activity. Complete the table.

Go Scuba Diving!

Would you like to go scuba diving?

A new scuba diving course is starting at the Olympia Sports Centre on 4th March. It's a six-week course and it's for beginners. There's a two-hour lesson every Thursday from 6pm to 8pm.

To do the course you must:
- be over 16.
- be good at swimming.

Bring your swimsuit and a towel!

For more information call: Olympia Sports Centre, Telephone 01323 826404

What is the activity?	....
Where is the course?	....
When does it start?	....
How many weeks is it?	....
When are the lessons?	....
How old must you be?	....
What must you be good at?	....
What must you bring?	....

5 Think of a course for a dangerous activity and make notes.

What is the activity?	....
Where is the course?	....
When does it start?	....
How many weeks is it?	....
When are the lessons?	....
How old must you be?	....
What must you be good at?	....
What must you bring?	....

6 Make an advertisement for your course. Use your notes from question 4, and the advertisement on page 43, to help you.

Go ....

Would you like to go ....?

For more information call:

GRAMMAR CHECK

There is/there are: affirmative, negative, questions, and short answers

We use there is (or there's) and there are to talk about things and people in a place.
We use there's with a singular noun, and there are with a plural noun.

There's a storm.   *There are three big snakes behind him.*

Negative forms are there isn't and there aren't.

There isn't a boat.   *There aren't any pirates in Serendib.*

Question forms are Is there and Aren't there. We do not use contractions in short affirmative answers.

Is there a king in your country? No, there isn't.

Are there any elephants here? Yes, there are.

Is there a monster?   *Yes, there is.* ✔   *Yes, there's.* ✗

1 Complete the sentences with the affirmative or negative form of *there is/there are*.

In Baghdad, a) ..*there's*.. a young man. His name is Sinbad. Sinbad is rich and

b) .... lots of expensive things in his house. c) .... a nice table and

d) .... five big chairs. But e) .... any brothers or sisters in Sinbad's family

to watch and help him.

Every night, Sinbad's friends come to his house, and they eat and drink. After a year,

f) .... any money and Sinbad isn't rich. When his friends visit again, they are very

surprised because g) .... any nice things to eat!

2 Complete the questions with *Is there* or *Are there*. Then write correct short answers.

a ..*Are there*.. any women in Chapter 1?   *No, there aren't*

b .... a whale in Chapter 1?   ....

c .... any cannibals in Chapter 3?   ....

d .... a shopkeeper in Chapter 4?   ....

e .... any barrels in Chapter 5?   ....

f .... a sea monster in Chapter 6?   ....

GRAMMAR CHECK

Would like or like

We often use would like to offer things, to invite people, or to ask for things politely.

Would you like an apple, Sinbad? Yes, I'd like that red apple, please. ('d = would)

We also use would like (or 'd like) + infinitive to talk about specific things that people want to do.

He'd like to go on an adventure.   *They'd like to leave the island.*

Would like is more polite than want.

I'd like to eat something. (polite)   *I want to eat something.* (not polite)

We use like (without *would*) to talk in general about nice (or not nice) things.

Sinbad likes exciting adventures.

Do you like apples, Yasmin? No, I don't like them very much.

3 Choose the correct word or words to complete the sentences.

  a '**Would**/**Do** you like to buy this carpet?' asks the shopkeeper.

  b Sinbad is in Serendib, but **he'd like**/**he likes** to leave now.

  c '**I'd like**/**I like** Baghdad,' says Yasmin. 'It's very nice.'

  d 'Where is the nearest island?' asks Sinbad. '**I'd like**/
    I like to find it.'

  e '**Would**/**Does** Sinbad like his new house?' asks his
    friend.

  f **We'd**/**We like** adventure stories. We read a lot of
    them.

  g **Would**/**Do** they like to read this book now?

4 Write a sentence with *would like* or *like* that means the same as the first sentence.

  a Are you interested in football? Do you like football?

  b Do you want to see the new *Sinbad* film? ....

  c We're interested in whales. ....

  d I want a drink of water, please. ....

  e Is she interested in jewels? ....

  f We want to go to that island, please. ....

GRAMMAR CHECK

Demonstrative pronouns: this, that, these, and those

We use this and that with singular nouns.

This is a nice carpet.   *I know that ship.*

We use these and those with plural nouns.

What are these stones?   *Those pirates are bad.*

We use this and these for things that are near to us.

This isn't an island. It's a whale!   *Would you like to buy these jewels?*

We use that and those for things that are far from us.

Let's get in that boat!   *Why are those elephants following us?*

5 Complete the sentences with *this, these, that or those*.

a ....This.... is Sinbad's father. He is old and ill.

b .... are my new clothes – here!

c Look there! .... shopkeepers are going to Sinbad's house.

d 'I can talk to .... captain over there,' thinks Sinbad.

e 'Help! .... storm's bad!' cry the sailors.

f 'I like .... jewels in your hand,' says Sinbad.

g .... woman by me is Yasmin.

6 Choose the correct word or words to complete the sentences.

a Sinbad likes **that/those** carpets, so he buys them.

b **That/Those** girl is the monster's prisoner.

c Perhaps **that/those** elephants want to tell them something.

d **That/Those** snake wants to eat Sinbad.

e 'That/Those pirates are attacking our ship!' cries Yasmin.

f Sinbad follows **that/those** big, strange animal.

g Sinbad and Yasmin are helping **that/those** people.

GRAMMAR

Countable and uncountable nouns: some and any

We use some and any to talk about an indefinite quantity or number, when we cannot or do not want to say exactly how much or how many we are thinking of.

Sinbad buys some carpets.   *Now we don't need to kill any elephants.*

We use some in affirmative sentences with plural countable nouns and with uncountable nouns.

There are some jewels on the beach.   *There is some water on the boat.*

We use any in negative sentences with plural countable nouns and with uncountable nouns.

The sailors can't see any monsters.   *Sinbad hasn't got any money.*

7 **Complete the sentences with *some* or *any*.**

   a The sailors want to make a fire, but there isn't ...any... wood.

   b 'I'm a prisoner and I need .... help!' cries Yasmin.

   c Sinbad and Yasmin follow .... elephants to a cave.

   d At first, Sinbad can't fight the big snake because he hasn't got .... armour.

   e 'Oh, no!' says the captain. 'I can see .... pirates near the ship!'

   f Sinbad doesn't want .... adventures today. He needs to sit down.

8 **Look at the picture. Complete the sentences with *some* or *any* and the words in the box.**

houses	new clothes	snakes	water	~~people~~	money

   a There are .....some people.... .

   b There aren't ....

   c Sinbad and Yasmin are wearing

       ....

   d There isn't ....

   e Sinbad has got ....

   f There are ....

GRAMMAR CHECK

Exclamations with what

We use exclamations with what when we have strong feelings about something – for example, when we think that something is very good or very bad.

What a wonderful island!   *What a bad storm!*

We use What + a/an with singular countable nouns.

What a big snake!   *What an old ship!*

We use What (without a/an) with plural countable nouns and with uncountable nouns.

What beautiful jewels!   What cold water!

9 **Write sentences using *what*, *what a*, or *what an*.**

a strange / monster

    What a strange monster!

b nice / carpet

....

c expensive / jewels

....

d exciting / adventure

....

e long / snake

....

f angry / shopkeepers

....

g interesting / story

....

h important / people

....

i warm / fire

....

GRAMMAR CHECK

Suffixes: −er, −r, and −or

When we add the suffix −er to a verb or noun (or −r when the verb or noun ends in −e), we make a word for a person.

The man hunts elephants. He's a hunter.

Sinbad has a lot of wonderful adventures. He's an adventurer.

We can also make a word for a person by adding the suffix −or to a verb.

Sinbad sails from Baghdad. He's a sailor.

If the word ends in a short vowel + consonant, we usually double the consonant.

jewel − jeweller   run − runner   begin − beginner   (but visitor and listener)

10 **Add *−er, −r,* or *−or* to the words in the box. Use the words to complete the dialogues.**

| begin | photograph | ~~prison~~ | sleep | teach | visit | write |

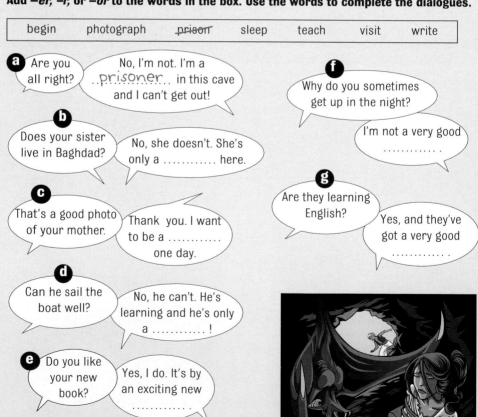

a Are you all right?

No, I'm not. I'm a ..prisoner.. in this cave and I can't get out!

b Does your sister live in Baghdad?

No, she doesn't. She's only a .... here.

c That's a good photo of your mother.

Thank you. I want to be a .... one day.

d Can he sail the boat well?

No, he can't. He's learning and he's only a .... !

e Do you like your new book?

Yes, I do. It's by an exciting new ....

f Why do you sometimes get up in the night?

I'm not a very good ....

g Are they learning English?

Yes, and they've got a very good ....

GRAMMAR CHECK

Making suggestions with let's and shall

We use let's (let us) + infinitive without to to make suggestions when the suggested action includes us.

Let's sit down and make a fire.   *Let's go onto that island.*

We can also use shall + I or we + infinitive without to to make suggestions.

Shall I tell you about my adventures?   Shall we go to the ship?

11 **Complete the sentences with *Let's*, *Shall I*, or *Shall we* and the words in the box.**

attack	be	~~help~~	leave	look	row	tell

a ' ..Shall I help.. you?' asks Sinbad. (shall I)

b '......................... you my name?' asks Sinbad.
(shall I)

c '......................... very careful!' says Yasmin. (let's)

d '......................... the monster and kill it?' asks
Sinbad. (shall we)

e '......................... the cave very quietly,' says Yasmin. (let's)

f '......................... for my ship,' says Sinbad. (let's)

g '......................... the boat to the ship?' asks Yasmin.
(shall we)

12 **Correct the sentences.**

a Shall we to buy these beautiful jewels?
     ....Shall we buy these beautiful jewels?............

b Let's stops the ship.
     ....

c Shall I throwing stones at the snake?
     ....

d Let's to run away from the pirates!
     ....

e Shall we to sail to Baghdad now?
     ....

DOMINOES Your Choice

Read *Dominoes* for pleasure, or to develop language skills. It's your choice.

Each *Domino* reader includes:
- a good story to enjoy
- integrated activities to develop reading skills and increase vocabulary
- task-based projects – perfect for CEFR portfolios
- contextualized grammar activities

Each *Domino* pack contains a reader, and an excitingly dramatized audio recording of the story

If you liked this *Domino*, read these:

Mulan

Retold by Janet Hardy-Gould

When the Emperor calls every man to join the army and fight the enemy, Mulan's father is old and ill, and cannot go. Wearing men's clothes and riding a horse, Mulan leaves her family and fights bravely for the Emperor in her father's place.

She is soon a hero for all the soldiers in the Chinese army. One of them, Ye Ming, is her best friend. But does he know that she is a woman? And can Mulan fall in love with a friend?

The Happy Prince

Oscar Wilde

The Happy Prince is a beautiful golden statue high up on a column in the city. Everyone loves him.

He feels sad about the city's poor people, but what can he do? He can't leave his column. Then the swallow arrives, and helps the Happy Prince to do many good things.

But what about the swallow's dream of flying to Egypt? And what does the Mayor do when the Happy Prince loses all his gold?

	CEFR	Cambridge Exams	IELTS	TOEFL iBT	TOEIC
Level 3	B1	PET	4.0	57-86	550
Level 2	A2–B1	KET-PET	3.0-4.0	–	390
Level 1	A1–A2	YLE Flyers/KET	3.0	–	225
Starter & Quick Starter	A1	YLE Movers	1.0–2.0	–	–

You can find details and a full list of books and teachers' resources on our website:
www.oup.com/elt/gradedreaders